The Little Dream by John Galsworthy

An Allegory in six scenes

Second Series Plays

John Galsworthy was born at Kingston Upon Thames in Surrey, England, on August 14th 1867 to a wealthy and well established family. His schooling was at Harrow and New College, Oxford before training as a barrister and being called to the bar in 1890. However, Law was not attractive to him and he travelled abroad becoming great friends with the novelist Joseph Conrad, then a first mate on a sailing ship.

In 1895 Galsworthy began an affair with Ada Nemesis Pearson Cooper, the wife of his cousin Major Arthur Galsworthy. The affair was kept a secret for 10 years till she at last divorced and they married on 23rd September 1905.

Galsworthy first published in 1897 with a collection of short stories entitled "The Four Winds". For the next 7 years he published these and all works under his pen name John Sinjohn. It was only upon the death of his father and the publication of "The Island Pharisees" in 1904 that he published as John Galsworthy.

His first play, The Silver Box in 1906 was a success and was followed by "The Man of Property" later that same year and was the first in the Forsyte trilogy. Whilst today he is far more well know as a Nobel Prize winning novelist then he was considered a playwright dealing with social issues and the class system. Here we publish Villa Rubein, a very fine story that captures Galsworthy's unique narrative and take on life of the time.

He is now far better known for his novels, particularly The Forsyte Saga, his trilogy about the eponymous family of the same name. These books, as with many of his other works, deal with social class, upper-middle class lives in particular. Although always sympathetic to his characters, he reveals their insular, snobbish, and somewhat greedy attitudes and suffocating moral codes. He is now viewed as one of the first from the Edwardian era to challenge some of the ideals of society depicted in the literature of Victorian England.

In his writings he campaigns for a variety of causes, including prison reform, women's rights, animal welfare, and the opposition of censorship as well as a recurring theme of an unhappy marriage from the women's side. During World War I he worked in a hospital in France as an orderly after being passed over for military service.

He was appointed to the Order of Merit in 1929, after earlier turning down a knighthood, and awarded the Nobel Prize in 1932 though he was too ill to attend.

John Galsworthy died from a brain tumour at his London home, Grove Lodge, Hampstead on January 31st 1933. In accordance with his will he was cremated at Woking with his ashes then being scattered over the South Downs from an aeroplane.

Index of Contents

Characters
Characters in the Dream
Voices and Figures in the Dream
Scene I
Scene II
Scene III
Scene IV
Scene V
Scene VI
John Galsworthy - A Short Biography
John Galsworthy – A Concise Bibliography

CHARACTERS
SEELCHEN, a mountain girl
LAMOND, a climber
FELSMAN, a glide

CHARACTERS IN THE DREAM
THE GREAT HORN   }
THE COW HORN   }   mountains
THE WINE HORN   }

THE EDELWEISS   }
THE ALPENROSE   } flowers
THE GENTIAN   }
THE MOUNTAIN DANDELION   }

VOICES AND FIGURES IN THE DREAM
COWBELLS
MOUNTAIN AIR
FAR VIEW OF ITALY
DISTANT FLUME OF STEAM
THINGS IN BOOKS
MOTH CHILDREN
THREE DANCING YOUTHS
THREE DANCING GIRLS
THE FORMS OF WORKERS
THE FORMS OF WHAT IS MADE BY WORK
DEATH BY SLUMBER
DEATH BY DROWNING
FLOWER CHILDREN
GOATHERD
GOAT BOYS

SCENE I

It is just after sunset of an August evening. The scene is a room in a mountain hut, furnished only with a table, benches. and a low broad window seat. Through this window three rocky peaks are seen by the light of a moon which is slowly whitening the last hues of sunset. An oil lamp is burning. **SEELCHEN**, a mountain girl, eighteen years old, is humming a folk-song, and putting away in a cupboard freshly washed soup-bowls and glasses. She is dressed in a tight-fitting black velvet bodice. square-cut at the neck and partly filled in with a gay handkerchief, coloured rose-pink, blue, and golden, like the alpen-rose, the gentian, and the mountain dandelion; alabaster beads, pale as edelweiss, are round her throat; her stiffened white linen sleeves finish at the elbow; and her full well-worn skirt is of gentian blue. The two thick plaits of her hair are crossed, and turned round her head. As she puts away the last bowl, there is a knock; and **LAMOND** opens the outer door. He is young, tanned, and good-looking, dressed like a climber, and carries a plaid, a ruck-sack, and an ice-axe.

LAMOND
Good evening!

SEELCHEN
Good evening, gentle Sir!

LAMOND
My name is Lamond. I'm very late I fear.

SEELCHEN
Do you wish to sleep here?

LAMOND
Please.

SEELCHEN
All the beds are full—it is a pity. I will call Mother.

LAMOND
I've come to go up the Great Horn at sunrise.

SEELCHEN [Awed]
The Great Horn! But he is impossible.

LAMOND
I am going to try that.

SEELCHEN

There is the Wine Horn, and the Cow Horn.

LAMOND
I have climbed them.

SEELCHEN
But he is so dangerous—it is perhaps—death.

LAMOND
Oh! that's all right! One must take one's chance.

SEELCHEN
And father has hurt his foot. For guide, there is only Hans Felsman.

LAMOND
The celebrated Felsman?

SEELCHEN [Nodding; then looking at him with admiration]
Are you that Herr Lamond who has climbed all our little mountains this year?

LAMOND
All but that big fellow.

SEELCHEN
We have heard of you. Will you not wait a day for father's foot?

LAMOND
Ah! no. I must go back home to-morrow.

SEELCHEN
The gracious Sir is in a hurry.

LAMOND [Looking at her intently]
Alas!

SEELCHEN
Are you from London? Is it very big?

LAMOND
Six million souls.

SEELCHEN
Oh! [After a little pause] I have seen Cortina twice.

LAMOND
Do you live here all the year?

SEELCHEN

In winter in the valley.

LAMOND
And don't you want to see the world?

SEELCHEN
Sometimes.

[Going to a door, she calls softly.

Hans!

[Then pointing to another door.

There are seven German gentlemen asleep in there!

LAMOND
Oh God!

SEELCHEN
Please? They are here to see the sunrise.

[She picks up a little book that has dropped from **LAMOND'S** pocket.

I have read several books.

LAMOND
This is by the great English poet. Do you never make poetry here, and dream dreams, among your mountains?

SEELCHEN [Slowly shaking her head]
See! It is the full moon.

[While they stand at the window looking at the moon, there enters a lean, well-built, taciturn young **MAN** dressed in Loden.

SEELCHEN
Hans!

FELSMAN [In a deep voice]
The gentleman wishes me?

SEELCHEN [Awed]
The Great Horn for to-morrow! [Whispering to him] It is the celebrated London one.

FELSMAN
The Great Horn is not possible.

LAMOND
You say that?   And you're the famous Felsman?

FELSMAN [Grimly]
We start at dawn.

SEELCHEN
It is the first time for years!

LAMOND [Placing his plaid and rucksack on the window bench]
Can I sleep here?

SEELCHEN
I will see; perhaps—

[She runs out up some stairs.

FELSMAN [Taking blankets from the cupboard and spreading them on the window seat]
So!

[As he goes out into the air. **SEELCHEN** comes slipping in again with a lighted candle.

SEELCHEN
There is still one bed. This is too hard for you.

LAMOND
Oh! thanks; but that's all right.

SEELCHEN
To please me!

LAMOND
May I ask your name?

SEELCHEN
Seelchen.

LAMOND
Little soul, that means—doesn't it?   To please you I would sleep with seven German gentlemen.

SEELCHEN
Oh! no; it is not necessary.

LAMOND [With a grave bow]
At your service, then.

[He prepares to go.

SEELCHEN
Is it very nice in towns, in the World, where you come from?

LAMOND
When I'm there I would be here; but when I'm here I would be there.

SEELCHEN [Clasping her hands]
That is like me but I am always here.

LAMOND
Ah! yes; there is no one like you in towns.

SEELCHEN
In two places one cannot be. [Suddenly] In the towns there are theatres, and there is beautiful fine work, and—dancing, and—churches—and trains—and all the things in books—and—

LAMOND
Misery.

SEELCHEN
But there is life.

LAMOND
And there is death.

SEELCHEN
To-morrow, when you have climbed—will you not come back?

LAMOND
No.

SEELCHEN
You have all the world; and I have nothing.

LAMOND
Except Felsman, and the mountains.

SEELCHEN
It is not good to eat only bread.

LAMOND [Looking at her hard]
I would like to eat you!

SEELCHEN
But I am not nice; I am full of big wants—like the cheese with holes.

LAMOND
I shall come again.

SEELCHEN
There will be no more hard mountains left to climb. And if it is not exciting, you do not care.

LAMOND
O wise little soul!

SEELCHEN
No. I am not wise. In here it is always aching.

LAMOND
For the moon?

SEELCHEN
Yes. [Then suddenly] From the big world you will remember?

LAMOND [Taking her hand]
There is nothing in the big world so sweet as this.

SEELCHEN [Wisely]
But there is the big world itself.

LAMOND
May I kiss you, for good-night?

[She puts her face forward; and he kisses her cheek, and, suddenly, her lips. Then as she draws away.

LAMOND
I am sorry, little soul.

SEELCHEN
That's all right!

LAMOND [Taking the candle]
Dream well! Goodnight!

SEELCHEN [Softly]
Good-night!

FELSMAN [Coming in from the air, and eyeing them]
It is cold—it will be fine.

[**LAMOND** still looking back goes up the stairs; and **FELSMAN** waits for him to pass.

SEELCHEN [From the window seat]
It was hard for him here. I thought.

[He goes up to her, stays a moment looking down then bends and kisses her hungrily.

SEELCHEN
Art thou angry?

[He does not answer, but turning out the lamp, goes into an inner room.

[SEELCHEN sits gazing through the window at the peaks bathed in full moonlight. Then, drawing the blankets about her, she snuggles doom on the window seat.

SEELCHEN [In a sleepy voice]
They kissed me—both.

[She sleeps.

The scene falls quite dark

SCENE II

The scene is slowly illumined as by dawn. **SEELCHEN** is still lying on the window seat. She sits up, freeing her face and hands from the blankets, changing the swathings of deep sleep for the filmy coverings of a dream. The wall of the hut has vanished; there is nothing between her and the three mountains veiled in mist, save a through of darkness. There, as the peaks of the mountains brighten, they are seen to have great faces.

SEELCHEN
Oh! They have faces!

[The face of **THE WINE HORN** is the profile of a beardless youth. The face of **THE COW HORN** is that of a mountain shepherd. solemn, and broom, with fierce black eyes, and a black beard. Between them **THE GREAT HORN**, whose hair is of snow, has a high. beardless visage, as of carved bronze, like a male sphinx, serene, without cruelty. Far down below the faces of the peaks. above the trough of darkness, are peeping out the four little heads of the flowers of **EDELWEISS**, and **GENTIAN, MOUNTAIN DANDELION**, and **ALPENROSE**; on their heads are crowns made of their several flowers, all powdered with dewdrops; and when **THE FLOWERS** lift their child-faces little tinkling bells ring.

[All around the peaks there is nothing but blue sky.

EDELWEISS [In a tiny voice]
Would you? Would you? Would you? Ah! ha!

GENTIAN, MOUNTAIN DANDELION, ALPENROSE [With their bells ranging enviously]
Oo-oo-oo!

[From behind **THE COW HORN** are heard the voices of **COWBELLS** and **MOUNTAIN AIR**:

"Clinkel-clink! Clinkel-clink!"

"Mountain air! Mountain air!"

[From behind **THE WINE HORN** rise the rival voices **Of VIEW OF ITALY, FLUME OF STEAM**, and **THINGS IN BOOKS**:

"I am Italy! Italy!"

"See me—steam in the distance!"

"O remember the things in books!"

[And all call out together, very softly, with **THE FLOWERS** ringing their bells. Then far away like an echo comes a sighing:

"Mountain air! Mountain air!"

[And suddenly the Peak of **THE COW HORN** speaks in a voice as of one unaccustomed.

THE COW HORN
Amongst kine and my black-brown sheep I Live; I am silence, and monotony; I am the solemn hills. I am fierceness, and the mountain wind; clean pasture, and wild rest. Look in my eyes, love me alone!

SEELCHEN [Breathless]
The Cow Horn! He is speaking for Felsman and the mountains. It is the half of my heart!

[**THE FLOWERS** laugh happily.

THE COW HORN
I stalk the eternal hills—I drink the mountain snows. My eyes are the colour of burned wine; in them lives melancholy. The lowing of the kine, the wind, the sound of falling rocks, the running of the torrents; no other talk know I. Thoughts simple, and blood hot, strength huge—the cloak of gravity.

SEELCHEN
Yes. yes! I want him. He is strong!

[The voices of **COWBELLS** and **MOUNTAIN AIR** cry out together:

"Clinkel-clink! Clinkel-clink!"

"Mountain air! Mountain air!"

THE COW HORN
Little soul! Hold to me! Love me! Live with me under the stars!

SEELCHEN [Below her breath]
I am afraid.

[And suddenly the Peak of **THE WINE HORN** speaks in a youth's voice.

THE WINE HORN
I am the will o' the wisp that dances thro' the streets; I am the cooing dove of Towns, from the plane trees and the chestnuts' shade. From day to day all changes, where I burn my incense to my thousand little gods. In white palaces I dwell, and passionate dark alleys. The life of men in crowds is mine—of lamplight in the streets at dawn. [Softly] I have a thousand loves and never one too long; for I am nimbler than your heifers playing in the sunshine.

THE FLOWERS, ringing in alarm, cry:
"We know them!"

THE WINE HORN
I hear the rustlings of the birth and death of pleasure; and the rattling of swift wheels. I hear the hungry oaths of men; and love kisses in the airless night. Without me, little soul, you starve and die,

SEELCHEN
He is speaking for the gentle Sir, and the big world of the Town. It pulls my heart.

THE WINE HORN
My thoughts surpass in number the flowers in your meadows; they fly more swiftly than your eagles on the wind. I drink the wine of aspiration, and the drug of disillusion. Thus am I never dull!

The voices of **VIEW OF ITALY**, **FLUME OF STEAM**, and **THINGS IN BOOKS** are heard calling out together:

"I am Italy, Italy!"

"See me—steam in the distance!"

"O remember, remember!"

THE WINE HORN
Love me, little soul! I paint life fifty colours. I make a thousand pretty things! I twine about your heart!

SEELCHEN
He is honey!

THE FLOWERS ring their bells jealously and cry:

"Bitter! Bitter!"

THE COW HORN
Stay with me, Seelchen! I wake thee with the crystal air.

[The voices of **COWBELLS** and **MOUNTAIN AIR** tiny out far away:

"Clinkel-clink! Clinkel-clink!"

"Mountain air! Mountain air!"

[And **THE FLOWERS** laugh happily.

THE WINE HORN
Come with me, Seelchen! My fan, Variety, shall wake you!

The voices of **VIEW OF ITALY, FLUME OF STEAM** and **THINGS IN BOOKS** chant softly:

"I am Italy! Italy!"

"See me—steam in the distance!"

"O remember, remember!"

And **THE FLOWERS** moan.

SEELCHEN [In grief]
My heart! It is torn!

THE WINE HORN
With me, little soul, you shall race in the streets. and peep at all secrets. We will hold hands, and fly like the thistle-down.

MOUNTAIN DANDELION
My puff-balls fly faster!

THE WINE HORN
I will show you the sea.

GENTIAN
My blue is deeper!

THE WINE HORN
I will shower on you blushes.

ALPENROSE
I can blush redder!

THE WINE HORN
Little soul, listen! My Jewels! Silk! Velvet!

EDELWEISS
I am softer than velvet!

THE WINE HORN [Proudly]
My wonderful rags!

THE FLOWERS [Moaning]

Of those we have none.

SEELCHEN
He has all things.

THE COW HORN
Mine are the clouds with the dark silvered wings; mine are the rocks on fire with the sun; and the dewdrops cooler than pearls. Away from my breath of snow and sweet grass, thou wilt droop, little soul.

THE WINE HORN
The dark Clove is my fragrance!

[**THE FLOWERS** ring eagerly, and turning up their faces, cry:

"We too, smell sweet."

But the voices of **VIEW OF ITALY, FLUME OF STEAM,** and **THINGS IN BOOKS** cry out:

"I am Italy! Italy!"

"See me—steam in the distance!"

"O remember! remember!"

SEELCHEN [Distracted]
Oh! it is hard!

THE COW HORN
I will never desert thee.

THE WINE HORN
A hundred times I will desert you, a hundred times come back, and kiss you.

SEELCHEN [Whispering]
Peace for my heart!

THE COW HORN
With me thou shalt lie on the warm wild thyme.

[**THE FLOWERS** laugh happily.

THE WINE HORN
With me you shall lie on a bed of dove's feathers.

[**THE FLOWERS** moan.

THE WINE HORN
I will give you old wine.

THE COW HORN
I will give thee new milk.

THE WINE HORN
Hear my song!

[From far away comes the sound as of mandolins.

SEELCHEN [Clasping her breast]
My heart—it is leaving me!

THE COW HORN
Hear my song!

[From the distance floats the piping of a Shepherd's reed.

SEELCHEN [Curving her hand at her ears]
The piping! Ah!

THE COW HORN
Stay with me, Seelchen!

THE WINE HORN
Come with me, Seelchen!

THE COW HORN
I give thee certainty!

THE WINE HORN
I give you chance!

THE COW HORN
I give thee peace.

THE WINE HORN
I give you change.

THE COW HORN
I give thee stillness.

THE WINE HORN
I give you voice.

THE COW HORN
I give thee one love.

THE WINE HORN

I give you many.

SEELCHEN [As if the words were torn from her heart]
Both, both—I will love!

[And suddenly the **Peak of THE GREAT HORN** speaks.

THE GREAT HORN
And both thou shalt love, little soul! Thou shalt lie on the hills with Silence; and dance in the cities with Knowledge. Both shall possess thee! The sun and the moon on the mountains shall burn thee; the lamps of the town singe thy wings. small Moth! Each shall seem all the world to thee, each shall seem as thy grave! Thy heart is a feather blown from one mouth to the other. But be not afraid! For the life of a man is for all loves in turn. 'Tis a little raft moored, then sailing out into the blue; a tune caught in a hush, then whispering on; a new-born babe, half courage and half sleep. There is a hidden rhythm. Change. Quietude. Chance. Certainty. The One. The Many. Burn on—thou pretty flame, trying to eat the world! Thou shaft come to me at last, my little soul!

[**THE VOICES** and **THE FLOWER-BELLS** peal out.

[**SEELCHEN**, enraptured, stretches her arms to embrace the sight and sound, but all fades slowly into dark sleep.

SCENE III

The dark scene again becomes glamorous. **SEELCHEN** is seen with her hand stretched out towards the Piazza of a little town, with a plane tree on one side, a wall on the other, and from the open doorway of an Inn a pale path of light. Over the Inn hangs a full golden moon. Against the wall, under the glimmer of a lamp, leans a youth with the face of **THE WINE HORN**, in a crimson dock, thrumming a mandolin, and singing:

"Little star soul
Through the frost fields of night
Roaming alone, disconsolate—
From out the cold
I call thee in
Striking my dark mandolin
Beneath this moon of gold."

[From the Inn comes a burst of laughter, and the sound of dancing.

SEELCHEN [Whispering]
It is the big world!

[The **Youth of THE WINE HORN** sings on:

"Pretty grey moth,

Where the strange candles shine,
Seeking for warmth, so desperate—
Ah! fluttering dove
I bid thee win
Striking my dark mandolin
The crimson flame of love."

SEELCHEN [Gazing enraptured at the Inn]
They are dancing!

[As **SHE** speaks, from either side come moth-children, meeting and fluttering up the path of light to the Inn doorway; then wheeling aside, they form again, and again flutter forward.

SEELCHEN [Holding out her hands]
They are real! Their wings are windy.

[The **Youth of THE WINE HORN** sings on;

"Lips of my song,
To the white maiden's heart
Go ye, and whisper, passionate.
These words that burn
'O listening one!
Love that flieth past is gone
Nor ever may return!'"

[**SEELCHEN** runs towards him—but the light above him fades; he has become shadow. She turns bewildered to the dancing moth-children —but they vanish before her. At the door of the Inn stands **LAMOND** in a dark cloak.

SEELCHEN
It is you!

LAMOND
Without my little soul I am cold. Come!

[He holds out his arms to her.

SEELCHEN
Shall I be safe?

LAMOND
What is safety? Are you safe in your mountains?

SEELCHEN
Where am I, here?

LAMOND

The Town.

[Smiling, he points to the doorway. And silent as shadows there come dancing out, two by two, **TWO GIRLS** and **TWO YOUTHS**. The first girl is dressed in white satin and jewels; and the first youth in black velvet. The second girl is in rags, and a shawl; and the second youth in shirt and corduroys. They dance gravely, each couple as if in a world apart.

SEELCHEN [Whispering]
In the mountains all dance together. Do they never change partners?

LAMOND
How could they, little one? Those are rich, these poor. But see!

[A **CORYBANTIC COUPLE** come dancing forth. The girl has bare limbs. a flame-coloured shift, and hair bound with red flowers; the youth wears a panther-skin. They pursue not only each other but the other girls and youths. For a moment all is a furious medley. Then the **CORYBANTIC COUPLE** vanish into the Inn, and the first two couples are left, slowly, solemnly dancing, apart from each other as before.

SEELCHEN [Shuddering]
Shall I one day dance like that?

[The **Youth of THE WINE HORN** appears again beneath the lamp. He strikes a loud chord; then as **SEELCHEN** moves towards that sound the lamp goes out; there is again only blue shadow; but the couples have disappeared into the Inn, and the doorway has grown dark.

SEELCHEN
Ah! What I do not like, he will not let me see.

LAMOND
Will you not come, then, little soul?

SEELCHEN
Always to dance?

LAMOND
Not so!

[The shutters of the houses are suddenly thrown wide. In a lighted room on one aide of the Inn are seen **TWO PALE MEN** and a **WOMAN**, amongst many clicking machines. On the other side of the Inn, in a forge, are visible two women and a man, but half clothed, making chains.

SEELCHEN [Recoiling from both sights, in turn]
How sad they look—all! What are they making?

[In the dark doorway of the Inn a light shines out, and in it is seen a **FIGURE**, visible only from the waist up, clad in gold-cloth studded with jewels, with a flushed complacent face, holding in one hand a glass of golden wine.

SEELCHEN
It is beautiful. What is it?

LAMOND
Luxury.

SEELCHEN
What is it standing on? I cannot see.

[Unseen, **THE WINE HORN'S** mandolin twangs out.

LAMOND
For that do not look, little soul.

SEELCHEN
Can it not walk?

[He shakes his head.

Is that all they make here with their sadness?

[But again the mandolin twangs out; the shutters fall over the houses; the door of the Inn grows dark.

LAMOND
What is it, then, you would have? Is it learning? There
are books here, that, piled on each other, would reach to the stars!

[But **SEELCHEN** shakes her head.

There is religion so deep that no man knows what it means.

[But **SEELCHEN** shakes her head.

There is religion so shallow, you may have it by turning a handle. We have everything.

SEELCHEN
Is God here?

LAMOND
Who knows? Is God with your goats?

[But **SEELCHEN** shakes her head.

What then do you want?

SEELCHEN
Life.

[The mandolin twangs out.

LAMOND [Pointing to his breast]
There is but one road to life.

SEELCHEN
Ah! but I do not love.

LAMOND
When a feather dies, is it not loving the wind—the unknown? When the day brings not new things, we are children of sorrow. If darkness and light did not change, could we breathe? Child! To live is to love, to love is to live-seeking for wonder.

[And as she draws nearer.

See! To love is to peer over the edge, and, spying the little grey flower, to climb down! It has wings; it has flown—again you must climb; it shivers, 'tis but air in your hand—you must crawl, you must cling, you must leap, and still it is there and not there—for the grey flower flits like a moth, and the wind of its wings is all you shall catch. But your eyes shall be shining, your cheeks shall be burning, your breast shall be panting—Ah! Little heart!

[The scene falls darker.

And when the night comes—there it is still, thistledown blown on the dark, and your white hands will reach for it, and your honey breath waft it, and never, never, shall you grasp that wanton thing—but life shall be lovely.

[His voice dies to a whisper. He stretches out his arms.

SEELCHEN [Touching his breast]
I will come.

LAMOND [Drawing her to the dark doorway]
Love me!

SEELCHEN
I love!

[The mandolin twangs out, the doorway for a moment is all glamorous; and they pass through. Illumined by the glimmer of the lamp the **Youth of THE WINE HORN** is seen again. And slowly to the chords of his mandolin he begins to sing:

"The windy hours through darkness fly
Canst hear them little heart?
New loves are born, and old loves die,
And kissing lips must part.

"The dusky bees of passing years

Canst see them, soul of mine—
From flower and flower supping tears,
And pale sweet honey wine?

[His voice grown strange and passionate.

"O flame that treads the marsh of time.
Flitting for ever low.
Where, through the black enchanted slime.
We, desperate, following go
Untimely fire, we bid thee stay!
Into dark air above.
The golden gipsy thins away—
So has it been with love!"

[While he is singing, the moon grows pale, and dies. It falls dark, save for the glimmer of the lamp beneath which he stands. But as his song ends, the dawn breaks over the houses, the lamp goes out—**THE WINE HORN** becomes shadow. Then from the doorway of the Inn, in the shrill grey light **SEELCHEN** comes forth. She is pale, as if wan with living; her eyes like pitch against the powdery whiteness of her face.

SEELCHEN
My heart is old.

[But as she speaks, from far away is heard a faint chiming of **COWBELLS**; and while she stands listening, **LAMOND** appears in the doorway of the Inn.

LAMOND
Little soul!

SEELCHEN
You! Always you!

LAMOND
I have new wonders.

SEELCHEN [Mournfully]
No.

LAMOND
I swear it! You have not tired of me, that am never the same? It cannot be.

SEELCHEN
Listen!

[The chime of **THE COWBELLS** is heard again.

LAMOND [Jealously]

The music' of dull sleep! Has life, then, with me been sorrow?

SEELCHEN
I do not regret.

LAMOND
Come!

SEELCHEN [Pointing-to her breast]
The bird is tired with flying.

[Touching her lips.

The flowers have no dew.

LAMOND
Would you leave me?

SEELCHEN
See!

[There, in a streak of the dawn, against the plane tree is seen the **Shepherd of THE COW HORN**, standing wrapped in his mountain cloak.

LAMOND
What is it?

SEELCHEN
He!

LAMOND
There is nothing.

[He holds her fast.

I have shown you the marvels of my town—the gay, the bitter wonders. We have known life. If with you I may no longer live, then let us die! See! Here are sweet Deaths by Slumber and by Drowning!

[The mandolin twangs out, and from the dim doorway of the Inn come forth the shadowy forms. **DEATH BY SLUMBER**, and **DEATH BY DROWNING**. who to a ghostly twanging of mandolins dance slowly towards **SEELCHEN**. stand smiling at her, and as slowly dance away.

SEELCHEN [Following]
Yes. They are good and sweet.

[While she moves towards the Inn. **LAMOND'S** face becomes transfigured with joy. But just as she reaches the doorway. there is a distant chiming of bells and blowing of pipes, and the **Shepherd of THE COW HORN** sings:

"To the wild grass come, and the dull far roar
Of the falling rock; to the flowery meads
Of thy mountain home, where the eagles soar,
And the grizzled flock in the sunshine feeds.
To the Alp, where I, in the pale light crowned
With the moon's thin horns, to my pasture roam;
To the silent sky, and the wistful sound
Of the rosy dawns—my daughter, come!"

[While **HE** sings, the sun has risen; and **SEELCHEN** has turned, with parted lips, and hands stretched out; and the forms of death have vanished.

SEELCHEN
I come.

LAMOND [Clasping her knees]
Little soul! Must I then die, like a gnat when the sun goes down? Without you I am nothing.

SEELCHEN [Releasing herself]
Poor heart—I am gone!

LAMOND
It is dark.

[He covers his face with his cloak.

Then as **SEELCHEN** reaches the **Shepherd of THE COW HORN**, there is blown a long note of a pipe; the scene falls back; and there rises a far, continual, mingled sound of Cowbells, and Flower Bells, and Pipes.

SCENE IV

The scene slowly brightens with the misty flush of dawn. **SEELCHEN** stands on a green alp, with all around, nothing but blue sky. A slip of a crescent moon is lying on her back. On a low rock sits a brown faced **GOATHERD** blowing on a pipe, and the four Flower-children are dancing in their shifts of grey white and blue, rose-pink, and burnt-gold. Their bells are ringing as they pelt each other with flowers of their own colours; and each in turn, wheeling, flings one flower at **SEELCHEN**, who puts them to her lips and eyes.

SEELCHEN
The dew!

[She moves towards the rock'

Goatherd!

[But **THE FLOWERS** encircle him; and when they wheel away he has vanished. She turns to **THE FLOWERS**, but they too vanish. The veils of mist are rising.

SEELCHEN
Gone!

[She rubs her eyes; then turning once more to the rock, sees **FELSMAN** standing there, with his arms folded.

Thou!

FELSMAN
So thou hast come—like a sick heifer to be healed. Was it good in the Town—that kept thee so long?

SEELCHEN
I do not regret.

FELSMAN
Why then return?

SEELCHEN
I was tired.

FELSMAN
Never again shalt thou go from me!

SEELCHEN [Mocking]
With what wilt thou keep me?

FELSMAN [Grasping her]
Thus.

SEELCHEN
I have known Change—I am no timid maid.

FELSMAN [Moodily]
Aye, thou art different. Thine eyes are hollow—thou art white-faced.

SEELCHEN [Still mocking]
Then what hast thou here that shall keep me?

FELSMAN
The sun.

SEELCHEN
To burn me.

FELSMAN

The air.

[There is a faint wailing of wind.

SEELCHEN
To freeze me.

FELSMAN
The silence.

[The noise of the wind dies away.

SEELCHEN
Yes, it is lonely.

FELSMAN
Wait! And the flowers shall dance to thee.

[And to a ringing of their bells. **THE FLOWERS** come dancing; till, one by one, they cease, and sink down, nodding, falling asleep.

SEELCHEN
See! Even they grow sleepy here!

FELSMAN
I will call the goats to wake them.

[**THE GOATHERD** is seen again sitting upright on his rock and piping. And there come four little brown, wild-eyed, naked BOYS, with Goat's legs and feet, who dance gravely in and out of The Sleeping Flowers; and **THE FLOWERS** wake, spring up, and fly. Till each Goat, catching his flower has vanished, and THE **GOATHERD** has ceased to pipe, and lies motionless again on his rock.

FELSMAN
Love me!

SEELCHEN
Thou art rude!

FELSMAN
Love me!

SEELCHEN
Thou art grim!

FELSMAN
Aye. I have no silver tongue. Listen! This is my voice.

[Sweeping his arm round all the still alp.

It is quiet. From dawn to the first star all is fast.

[Laying his hand on her heart.

And the wings of the birds shall be still.

SEELCHEN [Touching his eyes]
Thine eyes are fierce. In them I see the wild beasts crouching. In them I see the distance. Are they always fierce?

FELSMAN
Never—to look on thee, my flower.

SEELCHEN [Touching his hands]
Thy hands are rough to pluck flowers.

[She breaks away from him to the rock where **THE GOATHERD** is lying.

See! Nothing moves! The very day stands still. Boy!

[But **THE GOATHERD** neither stirs nor answers.

He is lost in the blue. [Passionately] Boy! He will not answer me. No one will answer me here.

FELSMAN [With fierce longing]
Am I then no one?

SEELCHEN
Thou?

[The scene darkens with evening.

See! Sleep has stolen the day! It is night already.

[There come the female shadow forms of **SLEEP**, in grey cobweb garments, waving their arms drowsily, wheeling round her.

SEELCHEN
Are you Sleep? Dear Sleep!

[Smiling, she holds out her arms to **FELSMAN.** He takes her swaying form. They vanish, encircled by the forms of **SLEEP**. It is dark, save for the light of the thin horned moon suddenly grown bright. Then on his rock, to a faint gaping **THE GOATHERD** sings:

"My goat, my little speckled one.
My yellow-eyed, sweet-smelling.
Let moon and wind and golden sun

And stars beyond all telling
Make, every day, a sweeter grass.
And multiply thy leaping!
And may the mountain foxes pass
And never scent thee sleeping!
Oh! Let my pipe be clear and far.
And let me find sweet water!
No hawk nor udder-seeking jar
Come near thee, little daughter!
May fiery rocks defend, at noon,
Thy tender feet from slipping!
Oh! hear my prayer beneath the moon—
Great Master, Goat-God—skipping!"

[There passes in the thin moonlight the Goat-Good Pan; and with a long wail of the pipe **THE GOATHERD BOY** is silent. Then the moon fades, and all is black; till, in the faint grisly light of the false dawn creeping up, **SEELCHEN** is seen rising from the side of the sleeping **FELSMAN. THE GOATHERD BOY** has gone; but by the rock stands the **Shepherd of THE COW HORN** in his dock.

SEELCHEN
Years, years I have slept. My spirit is hungry.

[Then as she sees the **Shepherd of THE COW HORN** standing there.

I know thee now—Life of the earth—the smell of thee, the sight of thee, the taste of thee, and all thy music. I have passed thee and gone by.

[She moves away.

FELSMAN [Waking]
Where wouldst thou go?

SEELCHEN
To the edge of the world.

FELSMAN [Rising and trying to stay her]
Thou shalt not leave me!

[But against her smiling gesture he struggles as though against solidity.

SEELCHEN
Friend! The time is on me.

FELSMAN
Were my kisses, then, too rude? Was I too dull?

SEELCHEN
I do not regret.

[The **Youth of THE WINE HORN** is seen suddenly standing opposite the motionless **Shepherd of THE COW HORN**; and his mandolin twangs out.

FELSMAN
The cursed music of the Town! Is it back to him thou wilt go?

[Groping for sight of the hated figure.

I cannot see.

SEELCHEN
Fear not! I go ever onward.

FELSMAN
Do not leave me to the wind in the rocks! Without thee love is dead, and I must die.

SEELCHEN
Poor heart! I am gone.

FELSMAN [Crouching against the rock]
It is cold.

[At the blowing of the Shepherd's pipe, **THE COW HORN** stretches forth his hand to her. The mandolin twangs out, and **THE WINE HORN** holds out his hand. She stands unmoving.

SEELCHEN
Companions. I must go. In a moment it will be dawn.

[In Silence **THE COW HORN** and **THE WINE HORN**, cover their faces. The false dawn dies. It falls quite dark.

SCENE V

Then a faint glow stealing up, lights the snowy head of **THE GREAT HORN**, and streams forth on **SEELCHEN**. To either aide of that path of light, like shadows. **THE COW HORN** and **THE WINE HORN** stand with cloaked heads.

SEELCHEN
Great One! I come!

[The Peak of **THE GREAT HORN** speaks in a far-away voice, growing, with the light, clearer and stronger.

Wandering flame, thou restless fever
Burning all things, regretting none;
The winds of fate are stilled for ever—

Thy little generous life is done.
And all its wistful wonderings cease!
Thou traveller to the tideless sea,
Where light and dark, and change and peace,
Are One—Come, little soul, to MYSTERY!

[**SEELCHEN** falling on her knees, bows her head to the ground. The glow slowly fades till the scene is black.

SCENE VI

Then as the blackness lifts, in the dim light of the false dawn filtering through the window of the mountain hut. **LAMOND** and **FELSMAN** are seen standing beside **SEELCHEN** looking down at her asleep on the window seat.

FELSMAN [Putting out his hand to wake her]
In a moment it will be dawn.

[She stirs, and her lips move, murmuring.

LAMOND
Let her sleep. She's dreaming.

[**FELSMAN** raises a lantern, till its light falls on her face. Then the **TWO MEN** move stealthily towards the door, and, as she speaks, pass out.

SEELCHEN [Rising to her knees, and stretching out her hands with ecstasy]
Great One. I come!

[Waking, she looks around, and struggles to her feet.

My little dream!

[Through the open door, the first flush of dawn shows in the sky. There is a sound of goat-bells passing.

The curtain falls.

John Galsworthy – A Short Biography

John Galsworthy, eldest son of John Galsworthy (1817-1904), a solicitor and company director of Old Jewry, London, and Blanche Bailey (1835-1915), daughter of Charles Bartleet, a needlemaker in Redditch. His father's ancestors originated in Wembury, near Plymouth in England, and Galsworthy, for whom family origins were of significant importance, maintained a close connection with Devon. His more immediate family were considerably wealthy and well established in the shipping industry, and owned a fine estate in Kingston-upon-Thames called Parkfield, where Galsworthy was born on the 14th

August 1867. At the age of nine he began education at Saugeen, a Bournemouth preparatory school, before starting at Harrow school in 1881 where he remained until 1886, distinguishing himself as an athlete.

His education at Harrow being successful enough to gain him entrance to Oxford, he began at New College to read law and gained a second-class degree with honours in 1889. Following Lincoln's Inn he was called to the bar in 1890. Despite this recognition he realised that he was not keen to actually begin practising law and so he resolved instead to look after the family's shipping business while specialising himself in Marine Law. This decision saw him take to the seas to destinations such as Vancouver, Island and South AFrica, though it was at the age of twenty-five on one particular journey to Australia, motivated by an (unfulfilled) intention to meet Robert Louis Stevenson on Samoa that he would being to realise fully his literary interests: though he was not considering becoming a writer at this time, his enjoyment of literature was enough to encourage an attempt at meeting a great writer and eventually enabled one of the most significant encounters of his life. He made the journey with his friend Edward Sanderson and, though he missed Stevenson, he met Joseph Conrad, a fellow future author famed for his novels which were often nautically themed. At the time Conrad was the first mate of the sailing-ship Torrens moored in the harbour of Adelaide, Australia; still very much focused on his ship-borne career, he was yet to begin his writing in earnest.

Indeed, though neither knew at the time, both Conrad and Galsworthy were at similar junctures in their lives, their time spent as sea acting as a transitional period during which each found their literary calling. It is perhaps owing to this unknown common ground that they became close friends. During his time on the Torrens Galsworthy recorded several details, offering a frank and valuable characterisation of Conrad while also illuminating his own experiences as a student of Marine Law.

"I supposed to be studying navigation for the Admiralty Bar, would every day work out the position of the ship with the captain. On one side of the saloon table we would sit and check our observations with those of Conrad, who from the other side of the table would look at us a little quizzically."

On his return to England and the cessation of his nautical voyaging, Galsworthy began an affair with the wife of his first cousin, Major Arthur John Galsworthy. Ada Nemesis Pearson Cooper (1864-1956), the daughter of Emanuel Copper, an obstetrician from Norwich, remained married to the Major for ten years and the affair remained secret for its duration. In order to conceal the affair they took considerable pains to avoid suspicion. One such tactic was to stay in a secluded farmhouse called Wingstone in the village on Manaton on Dartmoor, in Devon. In Galsworthy's decision to choose Devon as the location for their clandestine rendezvous we see evidence of Galsworthy's affection for the place of his father's origin. It was only when, in 1905, she divorced the Major that their affair became known following their marriage on 23rd September of that year.

Galsworthy now took to writing sometime after having met Conrad and his career began in earnest when, in 1897, his first work, From the Four Winds, a volume of short stories, was published under the pseudonym John Sinjohn. He succeeded this in 1898 with Jocelyn, his first novel, and then his second in 1900, Villa Rubein. In 1901 he published a second volume of short stories, A Man of Devon, which was the last of his work to be published under pseudonym. The first of his work to be published under his own name was The Island Pharisees in 1904, a novel of social observation, seasoned with flashes of satire and propaganda. His decision to write under his own name is arguably owing to the recent death of his father, either as a mark of respect to his name or because now he was able to publish freely without incurring the possibility of paternal disappointment at his choice of career. It also marked a shift in his professionalism; he had hitherto published with small, independent publishers, but The Island Pharisees was published by Heinemann, a far more established House and one with whom he remained for the duration of his writing career.

He arguably cemented his position and maturity as a writer when, in 1906, he saw the publication of both his first major play, The Silver Box, and the novel The Man of Property. Each was published to considerable critical acclaim, and to achieve both in such a short space of time was impressive. the Silver Box concerns the imbalance in the justice system with regards to criminals of differing class by contrasting the treatment of a poor thief and a rich thief, both of whom stole silver cigarette cases but for very different reasons. The complexity of individual experience when not dealt with in public is highlighted and questioned in a bravely critical manner; despite the clear issues it raises with class and privilege, the final night was attended by the Price and Princess of Wales. The Man of Property was the first novel in the famous The Forsyte Saga, a trilogy of novels with an 'interlude' between each one, written between 1906 and 1921. Dealing with the questions of status, class and materialism, The Man of Property introduces us to the Forsyte family, particularly Soames Forsyte, who is acutely aware of his status as 'new money' and equally keen to assert himself as a wealthy man. Jealous of his wife and desperate to own things in order to confirm his wealth to those observing him, he engineers a plan to keep his wife from her friends which backfires spectacularly when, instead of cutting her off, all Soames achieves is enabling her to have an affair. This drives Soames to terrible actions with terrible consequences, which Galsworthy depicts with confidence.

Very typically Edwardian, the novel focuses on conflict between property and art, and to a certain degree much of its emotional power is drawn from Galsworthy's own life, particularly his affair with Ada. Their rendezvous in the countryside of Devon mirror the manner in which Forsyte seeks to relocate his wife and; though theirs was a much healthier relationship, there are clear similarities. By examining the fragile nature of the class system and those moving within it Galsworthy offered an important perspective on the relationships between material wealth, personal happiness and obsession, and the manner in which these change over time. His contemporaries widely regarded the publication of this novel as marking the end of Victorianism. His friend Conrad praised it as "indubitably a piece of art" and, though the notoriously risqué D.H. Lawrence lamented the novel's timidity in the face of sexuality and sensuality, he considered it potentially "a very great novel, a very great satire".

Though he continued to write both plays and novels, it was his work as a playwright for which he was most celebrated by his contemporaries. Indeed, his next novel, The Country House, seems uncharacteristically unfocused, its satirical view of those belonging to the country set comparatively unremarkable and weakly characterised, while at times the tone of satire becomes one of ironic detachment. In 1909 he published Fraternity, an exploration of of the various connections between urban society and the social classes therein, though its representation of lower-class Londoners is utterly unconvincing and ill-informed. Remaining with the subject of the landed gentry and the society surrounding it, in 1915 he published The Freelands, which does not stray far from conservative discussions of capitalism, the rural economy and their interrelationship.

His drama, however, featured a convincingly muted realism, directed at a relatively small, educated and politically-aware audience. His social agenda is prevalent here too, and is represented in a simple and static manner producing arresting instances of high drama. This talent for creating moments of captivating theatre is complimented by an instinctual sense of balance enabling his narratives to vacillate between their emotional high- and low-points, ultimately reaching conclusive equilibrium. This is particularly evident in one of his most popular plays, Strife, published in 1909 and examining the antagonists in a strike at a Cornish tin mine. In this, and in 1910's Justice, he approaches his subject with sympathy, irony and balance, which establishes a position of narrative authority while garnering the audiences trust that he is representing his characters and their motives justly. Justice condemns the use of solitary confinement in prisons, a reformist agenda which caught the liberality of his contemporary audiences along with the home secretary, Winston Churchill. Despite he was careful to disassociate himself with politics and professed himself apolitical, he and his work were nevertheless aligned with the views of the Liberal establishment. He spent much of the duration of the First World War working in a field hospital in France as an orderly having been passed over for military service.

Despite the popularity and brilliance of his work, it was only in 1920 that he had his first true commercial success with The Skin Game, a melodrama dealing with ethics, property and class. The play was adapted by Alfred Hitchcock in 1931. Galsworthy, meanwhile, had turned down a knighthood in 1918, considering his work not sufficient to be made a knight of the realm. He did, however, accept the Belgian Palmes d'Or in the following year. In 1920 he published the second novel in the Forsyte Saga, In Chancery, in which he resumes many of the themes of the first novel, focusing on the marital disharmony between Soames Forsyte and his wife. Katherine Mansfield considered it "a fascinating, brilliant book" in her review in The Atheneum. Then, in 1921, he was elected as the PEN International Literary Club's first president. The concluding novel to The Forsyte Saga, To Let was published in 1921 with a kind of peace being found between Forsyte and his now-ex wife, though he is left contemplating his losses and his greed. More ironic treatment of class confusions followed in Loyalties, bringing with it more popular success which lasted until 1926 and Escape, the last of his popular plays. Though he enjoyed popular success it was inconsistent and relatively small. His Collected Plays was published in 1929.

Over the course of time the appreciation of his work has gradually shifted from his plays to his novels, and particularly the detail and intricacy of his chronicle of English social difference, tension and pretension in The Forsyte Saga. Its success encouraged Galsworthy to revisit Soames Forsyte in a second trilogy, A Modern Comedy, which follows Soames's obsessive love of his daughter Fleur. In its three volumes, The White Monkey (1924), The Silver Spoon (1936) and Swan Song (1928) he examines the English commercial upper-middle class and its ideologies, its instinct to possess as its only way of distinguishing itself manifested in the poisonous materialism of Soames. Interestingly, this emergent social class which he so vehemently criticises is the very class from which he emerged. He witnessed first-hand its insularity, its chauvinism, its restrictive and oppressive morality, its stubborn imperialism and its materialism, and it is this experience which enables him to write so comfortably about it. Swan Song is widely considered among the best of Galsworthy's writing for the depth of its exploration of society and its heightened emotional subtlety. In 1929 he was appointed to the Order of Merit, despite having turned down a knighthood earlier. He spent his last years writing a third trilogy, End of the Chapter, beginning in 1931 with Maid in Waiting, Flowering Wilderness in 1932 and concluding with Over The River in 1933. These are significantly less coherent works and are indicative of his deteriorating health. Indeed, in 1932 he was awarded the Nobel Prize, though he was too ill to attend the ceremony.

Throughout the course of his career he received honorary degrees from the universities of St Andrews (1922), Manchester (1927), Dublin (1929), Cambridge (1930), Sheffield (1930), Oxford (1931), and Princeton (1931). In 1926 New College, Oxford, elected him as an honourary fellow. In photographs he is portrayed as handsome, fastidiously dressed and dignified. He was unusually compassionate and this saw him involved in several charitable and humane causes throughout the course of his life, including penal reforms, attacks on theatrical censorship and campaigning for animal rights. Though he spent the majority of the final seven years of his life at his home in Bury, West Sussex, it was at his home in

Hampstead, London, that he died of a brain tumour on 31st January, 1933, six weeks after having been too ill to attend the ceremony in honour of his receiving the Nobel Prize. According to demands made in his will he was cremated and his ashes scattered over the South Downs from an aeroplane. Also in his will was his wish to leave cottages to several of his astonished tenants. He is memorialised in Highgate 'New' Cemetery and in the cloisters of New College, Oxford, where he was an honourary fellow.

John Galsworthy – A Concise Bibliography

From the Four Winds, 1897 (as John Sinjohn)
Jocelyn, 1898 (as John Sinjohn)
Villa Rubein, 1900 (as John Sinjohn)
A Man of Devon, 1901 (as John Sinjohn)
The Island Pharisees, 1904
The Silver Box, 1906 (his first play)
The Man of Property, 1906 – First book of The Forsyte Saga (1922)
The Country House, 1907
A Commentary, 1908
Fraternity, 1909
A Justification for the Censorship of Plays, 1909
Strife, 1909
Fraternity, 1909
Joy, 1909
Justice, 1910
A Motley, 1910
The Spirit of Punishment, 1910
Horses in Mines, 1910
The Patrician, 1911
The Little Dream, 1911
The Pigeon, 1912
The Eldest Son, 1912
Quality, 1912
Moods, Songs, and Doggerels, 1912
For Love of Beasts, 1912
The Inn of Tranquillity, 1912
The Dark Flower, 1913
The Fugitive, 1913
The Mob, 1914
The Freelands, 1915
The Little Man, 1915
A Bit o' Love, 1915
A Sheaf, 1916
The Apple Tree, 1916
The Foundations, 1917
Beyond, 1917
Five Tales, 1918
Indian Summer of a Forsyte, 1918 – First interlude of The Forsyte Saga
Saint's Progress, 1919

Addresses in America, 1912
In Chancery, 1920 – Second book of The Forsyte Saga
Awakening, 1920 – Second interlude of The Forsyte Saga
The Skin Game, 1920
To Let, 1921 – Third book of The Forsyte Saga
A Family Man, 1922
The Little Man, 1922
Loyalties, 1922
Windows, 1922
Captures, 1923
Abracadabra, 1924
The Forest, 1924
Old English, 1924
The White Monkey, 1924 – First book of A Modern Comedy
The Show, 1925
Escape, 1926
The Silver Spoon, 1926 – Second book of A Modern Comedy
Verses New and Old, 1926
Castles in Spain, 1927
A Silent Wooing, 1927 – First Interlude of A Modern Comedy
Passers By, 1927 – Second Interlude of A Modern Comedy
Swan Song, 1928 – Third book of A Modern Comedy
The Manaton Edition, 1923–26 (collection, 30 vols.)
Exiled, 1929
The Roof, 1929
On Forsyte 'Change, 1930
Two Essays on Conrad, 1930
Soames and the Flag, 1930
The Creation of Character in Literature, 1931 (The Romanes Lecture for 1931).
Maid in Waiting, 1931 – First book of End of the Chapter (1934)
Forty Poems, 1932
Flowering Wilderness, 1932 – Second book of End of the Chapter
Autobiographical Letters of Galsworthy: A Correspondence with Frank Harris, 1933
One More River (originally Over the River), 1933 – Third book of End of the Chapter
The Grove Edition, 1927–34 (collection, 27 Vols.)
Collected Poems, 1934
Punch and Go, 1935
The Life and Letters, 1935
The Winter Garden, 1935
Forsytes, Pendyces and Others, 1935
Selected Short Stories, 1935
Glimpses and Reflections, 1937

www.ingramcontent.com/pod-product-compliance
Lightning Source LLC
Chambersburg PA
CBHW060105050426
42448CB00011B/2628